L ✳ ✳ ✳ ✳ ✳ ✳ ✳ ✳ ✳ ✳ ✳

CIVIL WAR

KATHLYN GAY   MARTIN GAY

Twenty-First Century Books
A Division of Henry Holt and Company
New York

Twenty-First Century Books
A Division of Henry Holt and Company, Inc.
115 West 18th Street
New York, NY 10011

Henry Holt® and colophon are trademarks of
Henry Holt and Company, Inc.
Publishers since 1866

Library of Congress Cataloging-in-Publication Data
Gay, Kathlyn.
Civil War / Kathlyn Gay and Martin Gay. — 1st ed.
p. cm. — (Voices from the past)
Includes bibliographical references (p.) and index.
1. United States—History—Civil War, 1861–1865—Juvenile literature.
[1. United States—History—Civil War, 1861–1865.] I. Gay, Martin, 1950–
II. Title. III. Series: Gay, Kathlyn. Voices from the past.
E468.G38 1995   95–13412
973.7—dc20   CIP
                                                                                        AC

ISBN 0–8050–2845–5
First Edition 1995

Printed in the United States of America
All first editions are printed on acid-free paper ∞.
10 9 8 7 6 5 4 3 2 1

Map by Vantage Art, Inc.
Cover design by Karen Quigley
Interior design by Kelly Soong

Cover: *The First Minnesota* by Don Troiani.
Photograph courtesy Historical Art Prints, Southbury, Conn.

Photo credits

pp. 8, 26, 35, 36, 37, 47, 53: The Bettmann Archive; p. 12: The Sofia Smith Collection, Smith College; pp. 18 (both), 55: North Wind Picture Archives; p. 19: Anne S. K. Brown Military Collection, Brown University; pp. 22, 30, 32, 52: *The Photographic History of the Civil War* in 10 volumes published in New York in 1912 by The Review of Reviews Co.; pp. 28, 40, 48: Culver Pictures; p. 42: *Harper's Weekly*, August 1, 1863; p. 44: National Archives; p. 45: National Park Service.

Contents

Acknowledgments

Some of the research for this series depended upon the special efforts of Dean Hamilton, who spent many hours locating primary source materials and other references on America's wars and sorting out appropriate stories among the many personal accounts available. Especially helpful was his work at the archival library of the University of South Florida at Tampa, researching for Spanish-American War and Civil War narratives. For the *World War I* title in this series, Dean also applied his special talents interviewing several of the few remaining veterans of WW I, obtaining their highly personal recollections, which the veterans allowed us to include. Thanks, Dean.

In addition, we would like to thank Lt. Col. (retired) John McGarrahan for locating narratives about personal experiences in the War of 1812, available in the archives at the Lilly Library, Indiana University, Bloomington, Indiana. We also thank Douglas Gay for obtaining narratives on the battle of Tippecanoe at the Tippecanoe County Historical Association in Lafayette, Indiana. Portions of these accounts are included in the *War of 1812* title in this series.

—Kathlyn Gay and Martin Gay

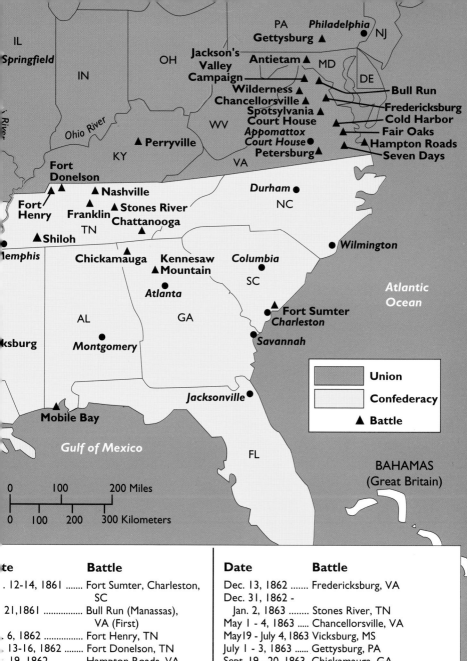

IL				PA	*Philadelphia*			
Springfield				Gettysburg ▲			NJ	
IN		OH	Jackson's	Antietam ▲	MD			
			Valley			DE		
			Campaign	Wilderness ▲			Bull Run	
				Chancellorsville ▲			Fredericksburg	
	Ohio River		WV	Spotsylvania ▲			Cold Harbor	
River				Court House			Fair Oaks	
		▲ Perryville		Appomattox			Hampton Roads	
	KY		VA	Court House ●			Seven Days	
Fort				Petersburg ▲				
Donelson								

Battles map labels:

- Fort Henry ▲
- Nashville ▲
- Stones River ▲
- Franklin
- Chattanooga ▲
- Shiloh ▲
- Durham ●
- NC
- Chickamauga ▲
- Kennesaw ▲ Mountain
- Columbia ●
- Wilmington ●
- Memphis
- SC
- Atlanta ●
- Atlantic Ocean
- AL
- GA
- Fort Sumter ▲
- Charleston ●
- ksburg
- Montgomery ●
- Savannah ●
- Jacksonville ●
- Mobile Bay ▲
- Gulf of Mexico
- FL
- BAHAMAS (Great Britain)

	Union
	Confederacy
▲	Battle

0   100   200 Miles
0   100   200   300 Kilometers

te	Battle	Date	Battle
. 12-14, 1861	Fort Sumter, Charleston, SC	Dec. 13, 1862	Fredericksburg, VA
21,1861	Bull Run (Manassas), VA (First)	Dec. 31, 1862 - Jan. 2, 1863	Stones River, TN
6, 1862	Fort Henry, TN	May 1 - 4, 1863	Chancellorsville, VA
13-16, 1862	Fort Donelson, TN	May19 - July 4, 1863	Vicksburg, MS
. 19, 1862	Hampton Roads, VA (*Monitor & Merrimac*)	July 1 - 3, 1863	Gettysburg, PA
. 6 - 7, 1862	Shiloh, TN	Sept. 19 - 20, 1863	Chickamauga, GA
ʷ 4 - June 9, 1862	Jackson's Valley Campaign, VA	Nov. 23 - 25, 1863	Chattanooga, TN
		May 5 - 6, 1864	Wilderness, VA
ʷ 31 - June 1, 1862	Fair Oaks, VA	May 8 - 19, 1864 ..	Spotsylvania Court House, VA
ₑ 25 - July 1, 1862	Seven Days, VA	June 1 - 3, 1864	Cold Harbor, VA
, 27 - 30, 1862	Bull Run (Manassas), VA (Second)	June 20, 1864 - Apr. 2, 1865	Petersburg, VA
t. 17, 1862	Antietam, MD	June 27, 1864	Kennesaw Mountain, GA
. 8, 1862	Perryville, KY	Aug. 5, 1864	Mobile Bay, AL
		Nov. 30, 1864	Franklin, TN
		Dec. 15 - 16, 1864	Nashville, TN

One

MONUMENTAL ISSUES

$\mathcal{R}$umors of war began to spread through the land. Companies of soldiers were being formed,"[1] wrote Céline Garcia, describing conditions in the United States during the year 1860, when she was ten years old. For most of her life, Céline lived in Louisiana with her French immigrant family. Her father was an officer of the local volunteer militia, and he and his friends had often talked of armed conflict.

Yet to Céline and many other children and adults of that time, "war was only a name." Few believed that people in the United States would actually take up arms against one another, which was what the "rumors of war" were about. Nevertheless, many Americans were well aware that the nation faced monumental issues. Some conflicts had been fermenting for decades and had divided people along sectional lines.

One basic disagreement focused on the rights of states to make decisions in their best interests, which had been an issue during the War of 1812, particularly among those who opposed the second war with the British. At the peak of the war, in 1814, New England lawmakers, who were members of the Federalist political party, wanted to amend the Constitution to guarantee more independence for the states. But before they could present their proposal in Washington,

D.C., the war ended. Afterward, many Americans, bolstered by victory and national pride, believed the Federalist lawmakers were foolish at best and treasonous at worst. As a result, the party lost power, setting the stage for new political parties to form.

THE MOST DIVISIVE ISSUE

New political parties did not necessarily ignore sectional or state interests, however. Such concerns became ever more important during the mid-1800s as people moved to the West and Southwest and settled those territories. In each territory, citizens voted on whether to join the Union as a "slave" or "free" state—that is, whether the new state would allow slavery or ban the practice. This became the most explosive issue in the nation, creating heated debate that led to violence in many parts of the country.

Debates over whether a state should join the Union
as a free or a slave state often led to violence.

Slavery had been introduced in North America during the time Europeans were establishing colonies. Although some Africans came to the early colonies as free people, from the 1600s on European traders captured people of African descent and, under brutal conditions, shipped their captives to North and South America and the Caribbean. Enslaved people were considered property and were sold like cattle. They had no rights and were forced to work for slave owners who called themselves "masters." Most white slave owners and others who supported slavery believed they had inherited mental and moral qualities superior to people of color—not only Africans but also people of mixed ancestry and Native Americans, many of whom were enslaved also.

Attempts have been made to prove the theory of racial superiority, but no scientific evidence has been able to support that notion. Nevertheless, this false view convinced many whites that they were justified in using forced labor. In the United States, slaves worked primarily on plantations in the South, providing economic benefits for many plantation owners. Although most Southerners were not slave owners, slaves were the backbone of the Southern economy.

OPPOSITION TO SLAVERY

Some Americans had opposed slavery from its beginnings, but the institution of slavery was allowed to continue when the U.S. Constitution was written in 1787. By the early 1800s, all states north of Maryland had either promised to free slaves or had passed laws that forbade slavery. In 1808, a federal law banned the import of slaves into the United States, but some traders defied the ban and smuggled slaves into the South, where slavery was legal.

People interested in various types of social reforms began to organize during the 1820s and 1830s. Among the reformers were those who wanted to abolish slavery—abolitionists, as they were called.

The abolitionist movement included many free blacks and escaped slaves such as Frederick Douglass and Sojourner Truth, who were active abolitionists long before most white reformers. Several black leaders joined forces with white abolitionists like William Lloyd Garrison of Massachusetts, who founded and published the antislavery newspaper the *Liberator* in 1831. The following year, he helped organize the New England Anti-Slavery Society and the American Anti-Slavery Society. Women, who led campaigns to gain civil rights for both women and blacks, also founded antislavery groups in New England towns and cities.

"LET IT BE ACCURSED"

Some proslavery Americans declared that slaves were well treated, but abolitionist Theodore D. Weld set out to prove that slave life was inhumane. He collected firsthand accounts about slave conditions, which he compiled in a 200-page document titled *American Slavery As It Is: Testimony of a Thousand Witnesses*. Published in 1839, the book sold more than 100,000 copies. In an introduction, Weld called on the nation to pronounce a sentence against slavery: "Let it be accursed. Let it be accursed," he wrote.

Most of the narratives in Weld's book were horror stories, particularly those that told how slaves were punished, as this excerpt from a relatively "mild" narrative of a former slave trader reveals:

> For the slightest offence, such as taking a hen's egg, I have seen them stripped and suspended by their hands, their feet tied together, a fence rail of ordinary size placed between their ankles, and then most cruelly whipped, until, from head

to foot, they were completely lacerated, a pickle made for the purpose of salt and water, would then be applied by a fellow-slave, for the purpose of healing the wounds as well as giving pain. Then taken down and without the least respite sent to work with their hoe.[2]

Weld's book and other published works like Harriet Beecher Stowe's *Uncle Tom's Cabin* that described the degradation of slave life riled people in the North. Some attacked the Southern lifestyle that supported slavery. Southerners reacted defensively, claiming that if slavery were banned, the Southern economy, which depended on forced gang labor, would be destroyed. That in turn would have adverse effects on the North, since Northern factories needed Southern-grown cotton and other raw materials to manufacture products.

Some Southerners feared that if slaves were freed, they would organize and attack whites in revenge against those who had enslaved and abused them. But slaves were seldom violent, although they often resisted slavery with work slow-downs or by destroying crops and tools. On a few occasions, some slaves staged uprisings, but their efforts failed to bring freedom; those who rebelled were usually caught and hanged. Still, each year about 1,000 slaves managed to escape. They often got help from abolitionists who operated a system of hideouts known as the Underground Railroad. This involved a network of people who worked in secret, often risking their own lives, to hide escapees or to lead them to safe places as they traveled from the South to freedom in Northern states, parts of the Midwest and West, and Canada.

Yet escaped slaves were still in great danger. Under pressure from Southern representatives, the U.S. Congress passed the Fugitive Slave Act of 1850, which legalized the capture of runaway slaves, who were then returned to

Harriet Tubman (far left) was a famous abolitionist
who helped slaves escape to the North.

bondage. Some slave owners hired vigilantes to go after escaped slaves, including those who had escaped to freedom years before. Posses sometimes kidnapped free blacks who were falsely identified as slaves.

RESISTANCE TO THE FUGITIVE SLAVE LAW

In 1854 one fugitive slave, Anthony Burns, was captured in Boston and imprisoned inside the courthouse. A group of citizens tried to break into the courthouse to free Burns, but the state militia and federal troops were called in to stand guard while a U.S. official pondered legal action.

Charlotte Forten, the sixteen-year-old granddaughter of James Forten, a free black and famous abolitionist, began a diary during that time. When the decision was made in favor of the slave owner, Charlotte expressed her scorn for a government that

> cowardly assembles thousands of soldiers to satisfy the demands of slaveholders; to deprive of his freedom a man ... whose sole offence is the color of his skin! And if resistance is offered to this outrage, these soldiers are to shoot down American citizens without mercy; and this ... on the very soil where the Revolution of 1776 began; in sight of the battle-field, where thousands of brave men fought and died in opposing British tyranny, which was nothing compared with the American oppression of to-day.[3]

Many people in the North and Midwest shared Charlotte's disgust for the oppressive effects of the Fugitive Slave Act. Throughout the 1850s, Northerners often defied the law, increasing tensions between the North and South. Many other incidents also contributed to the friction. One was the attempt by John Brown, a radical abolitionist from Kansas, to start a slave uprising at Harpers Ferry, Virginia (later West Virginia), in October 1859. The insurrection failed and state militia captured Brown. He was executed in December.

The following year, even more controversy erupted between the Northern and Southern sections of the country as people prepared to elect a president. Although some voters hoped that the right person would be elected to hold the nation together, the election campaigns revealed the deep discord in the nation over the issue of states' rights and slavery. The day would soon come when, as young Céline in Louisiana recalled, "A flag was brought to Ma to be altered . . . blue stripes to be inserted between the red and white bars"[4] to serve as a temporary flag for the local militia, a flag that no longer represented the United States.

Two

DISCORD AND DIVISION

*B*efore the presidential campaign of 1860, the political party system in the nation began to break down. Four major parties formed and all ran candidates for the presidency.

A Constitutional-Union Party organized to emphasize strict compliance with the U.S. Constitution and support for the Union. The Democratic Party split into two factions (or parties), one representing the North and the other the South. Both believed slavery should continue, but the Northern faction said the federal government had the right to restrict slavery in the territories. The Southern faction opposed federal intervention and threatened to secede and form a confederacy if states' rights were not honored by the federal government.

Only the Republican Party was antislavery, albeit in a token way. Republicans did not advocate ending slavery; rather they wanted to prevent its extension into the territories that had not yet become states.

None of the political parties appealed to the majority of abolitionists. As one black leader noted, "So far as the principles of freedom and the hopes of the black man are concerned, all these parties are barren and unfruitful; neither of them seeks to lift the negro out of his fetters."[1] Yet as the campaign wore on, abolitionists generally supported the Republican Party, because it was the only one to take any kind of antislavery position.

THE ELECTION OF LINCOLN

The Republican candidate, Abraham Lincoln, was never an abolitionist, although he considered slavery "an evil not to be extended" and hoped to stop its spread. His main concern during the campaign and after his election in November 1860 was to keep the United States together and prevent war. But many people were not certain that a man inexperienced in national affairs would be effective.

Theodore Upson, a fifteen-year-old living on a farm near the Indiana-Michigan border, kept a journal at that time and summed up in simple terms the general reaction to the new administration: "Well we have elected Lincoln for President and everybody seems to think its all right though some say it means trouble." [2]

In Congress, Southerners were sure Lincoln meant trouble. They felt that the "Black Republicans," as the party was frequently called, would violate states' rights, ban slavery, and destroy what they felt was a proud and genteel way of life. Many Southerners believed the only recourse was secession. In their view, if a state disagreed with the policies of the federal government, it had the right to leave the Union.

Not long after the election, Theodore read a letter from a family friend in Tennessee who described his state's plan to secede. The friend predicted that "all the slave states will pull out . . . they are going to leave peaceably if they can but if worst comes to worst The Gallant Sons of Tennessee will stand like a wall of fire around [Tennessee] to protect her homes her families and her property." [3]

SECESSION

Tennessee was not the first state to make a move, however. Four days after the election, U.S. senators from South Carolina resigned from Congress, and on December 20, three months before Lincoln's inauguration, the state seceded. Within six weeks, Mississippi, Florida, Alabama, Georgia, and Louisiana withdrew as well. By early February 1861, the six states had formed a new government called the Confederate States of America. In late February, Texas seceded and joined the Confederacy in March. Jefferson Davis, a graduate of West Point and former secretary of war under President Franklin Pierce, became president of the Confederacy.

When Lincoln was inaugurated on March 4, 1861, he still hoped to keep the Union intact. In his inaugural address, he said, "No state, upon its own mere motion, can lawfully get out of the Union." Based on the U.S. Constitution, he had the power to "hold, occupy, and possess the property and places belonging to the government." Nevertheless, Lincoln promised "dissatisfied fellow-countrymen" that the federal government would not attack them unless they became "the aggressors. *You* have no oath . . . to destroy the government, while *I* . . . have the most solemn one to 'preserve, protect, and defend' it," he said.[4]

But the Confederate states considered themselves a separate nation and the United States a foreign country that might soon attack. Thus, even before Lincoln took office, Confederate forces had seized U.S. forts, naval yards, post offices, and other buildings. To avoid bloodshed, federal troops turned over the facilities without a fight. Only Fort Sumter, built as an island in Charleston harbor in South Carolina, and a few smaller forts in the Confederacy were still under U.S. control.

THE FALL OF FORT SUMTER

Although federal forces held Fort Sumter in early April 1861, they were low on food and other supplies. Major Robert Anderson, the commander, had sent a request for help to Lincoln, and relief supplies were on the way. But Confederate President Jefferson Davis ordered an evacuation of the fort.

Major Anderson refused to leave, offering instead to surrender in two days, when the food would be gone. Since Confederate officers did not trust the Northerners, they refused to wait. Early on the morning of April 12, 1861, from their position on Charleston's waterfront, they fired their cannons across the harbor—the first shots of the war.

U.S. troops returned the fire, and the bombardment continued through that day and part of the next. The fort was nearly destroyed, supplies were gone, and Major Anderson was forced to surrender. On April 14, the Confederates allowed Anderson to take down his flag and sail with his troops to New York.

When news of the event reached the North, reaction was explosive. To most Northerners, the Rebels or Rebs, as the Confederates were known, were traitors; they had committed an act of treason by firing on the U.S. flag.

Theodore Upson was helping his father husk corn when an uncle rushed across the farm field to report the somber news. "Father got white and couldn't say a word," Theodore wrote in his journal. "We did not finish the corn and drove to the barn. Father left me to unload . . . and went to the house."[5] Theodore added that his father seemed to age ten years.

Even though the Civil War had begun, the Upsons and many others in the nation thought the war would last only a few months. Few believed the fighting would go on for four long years.

*After the two-day
bombardment of
Fort Sumter (top),
much of the fort
was in ruins
(bottom).*

THE NORTHERN CALL FOR VOLUNTEERS

After the surrender of Fort Sumter, Lincoln asked the
Northern states to provide 75,000 militiamen for a three-
month enlistment. A month later, he called for 40,000 more
recruits. He also declared a naval blockade on the ports of all
seceded states.

No matter what their political beliefs, most people in
the North rallied behind the president, fervently supporting
the Union. People in cities like Boston, New York, and
Philadelphia filled the streets to cheer on the volunteer regi-

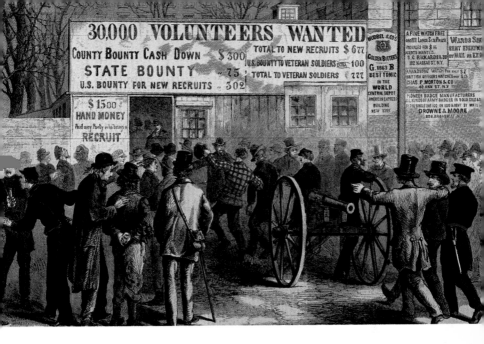

A recruiting hall in the North

ments that quickly organized. Those regiments included young men from nearly all walks of life. Some were fairly recent immigrants. They were part of the vast immigration that took place during the early part of the 1800s, when immigrants came from such countries as Germany, Ireland, England, Sweden, France, and Italy.

Rallies were held in many small towns and villages also, as speakers and recruiters signed up volunteers for battle. In his journal, Theodore Upson described a typical scene when a Michigan militia company paraded through his town:

> Some of us boys had a fife and drum and a flag and marched behind them. There was a speaker from away off some place and he told what the government was going to do to the Rebels and a lot of such talk and finally grabbed the flag ... waved it around and shouted: "On to Richmond" [capital of the Confederacy] ... people cheered and cheered.[6]

Although the minimum age for enlistees was eighteen, many boys between twelve and fifteen years old lied about their age in order to wear the Union blue, the federal uniform. And numerous boys eight to ten years of age who were runaways or orphans were allowed to tag along with the troops as mascots or unofficial drummers and fifers.

During the war, at least 400 women disguised as men also joined up. Because medical examinations were superficial, the gender of most female soldiers was not discovered unless they were wounded or died in battle.

Many free blacks hoped to serve in the Union forces, but they were not accepted at first. Lincoln insisted that the war was not an abolitionist war, so it had nothing to do with blacks. Some Northern officials claimed that blacks did not want to fight. Others believed that if blacks took up arms, they would try to massacre slave owners.

Nevertheless, black men formed companies and regiments so they would be ready if called. Alfred M. Green, a prominent black teacher and organizer in Philadelphia, was one of the first to discuss the recruitment of blacks into the Pennsylvania militia. In a letter to the *Philadelphia Press*, Green argued in late April 1861 that "hundreds of brawny ebony men are ready to fill up the ranks if the State will accept their services. Peril and war blot out all distinction of race and rank. These colored soldiers should be attached to the Home Guard."[7]

Other prominent black leaders strongly disagreed with Green's views, however. They were opposed to serving a nation that had failed to recognize them as citizens, even after their forefathers had proven their loyalty and bravery during the Revolution and the War of 1812. Many also worried that as soldiers they would be expected to fight slaves who might be forced to take up arms on the Confederate side.

SOUTHERN RECRUITS

The Confederates did force some slaves to serve, but blacks did not always remain loyal. In one instance, the crew of a Rebel gunboat consisted entirely of slaves, with three white officers in charge. The slaves were able to take over the ship while it was anchored in Charleston harbor and the officers were ashore. After secretly taking their families aboard, the slaves sailed out of the harbor, beyond Fort Sumter, and turned the gunboat over to the Union navy.

Confederates actively recruited warriors among the Choctaw, Chickasaw, Cherokee, Creek, and Seminole Nations, whose lands covered thousands of acres in the South. Except for the Seminole, these Indian nations had formed some ties with Southerners, including the adoption of slavery, and some warriors were enticed to join Confederate troops.

For the most part, though, the enlisted Rebels were, like the Yankees or Yanks, as the Northern troops were called, young white men and boys. They considered them-selves "common folk" loyal to a cause that to many in the South was a war for independence. Confederates also believed they had to protect their families and homes from foreign invaders—the Union forces.

During 1861, more than 100,000 volunteers signed up to fight for the Confederacy. Later, many more recruits came from states that seceded after the Confederacy was formed: North Carolina, Tennessee, Arkansas, and Virginia. The western portion of Virginia, however, did not want to be part of the Confederacy and in the fall of 1861 pulled away and formed its own state, which was admitted into the Union as West Virginia in 1863.

Some young men from the slave states that stayed with

More than 3,000 Indians fought for the North, but the Confederacy enlisted many more. These Indian sharpshooters were wounded at the Battle of Fredericksburg.

the Union also joined Rebel forces, as did a number of Northern military officers. At the same time, some in the South joined the Yanks. As people chose sides, they often found themselves in the tragic situation of fighting against family members, friends, and neighbors. In some cases, even though families split in their loyalties, members refused to take up arms against their brothers or friends.

The family of Judge Thomas Gibbes Morgan of Baton Rouge, Louisiana, faced this situation early in the war when the eldest of Morgan's five sons, Philip, declared allegiance to the Union. But Philip would not leave Louisiana or take up arms against his friends and relatives. However, a son-in-law of Morgan, Richard Drum, did join Union forces, although he was stationed in California and was never called to fight Southerners.

Townspeople often criticized the Morgan family for their divided loyalties. According to Morgan's daughter Sarah, family members were "vilified" because they "were unwilling to blackguard [insult]" federal troops who seized Baton Rouge in the spring of 1862. About that time, twenty-year-old Sarah Morgan began a diary and explained that she and others in her family did not agree with

> many of our friends in saying [federal officers] were liars, thieves, murderers, scoundrels, the scum of the earth. . . . I have a brother-in-law in the Federal army whom I love and respect as much as any one in the world, and shall not readily agree that his being a Northerner would give him an irresistible desire to pick my pockets, and take from him all power of telling the truth. No! There are few men I admire more than Major Drum, and I honor him for his independence in doing what he believes right. . . . Shall I acknowledge that the people we so recently called our brothers are unworthy of consideration, and are liars, cowards, dogs? Not I![8]

Although Sarah frequently defended individual federal officials, she often pointed out in diary entries that she despised the Union takeover of Southern towns. She believed the South should "fight until we win the cause so many have died for. I don't believe in Secession, but I do in Liberty. I want the South to conquer, dictate its own terms, and go back to the Union," she wrote.[9]

Whatever their loyalties, the war touched most people in the nation. For the first time photographs of the conflict's terrible destruction were displayed in major cities, and newspapers and magazines carried sketches of the maimed and dead in the battles. Worst of all, most families lost at least one member in the bloodiest war of the century. For example, three of Sarah's brothers served with Confederate forces and only one survived. Other families—North and South—lost all members who served in the military.

Three

"THE REAL WAR"

s young recruits marched off to battle, they seldom knew what to expect. The real horrors of war were yet to come, so in the spring of 1861 spirits were high among the new soldiers as well as those who sent them off to fight. "The towns people all turn out to see us off. Among them are Mothers, Fathers, sisters and brothers to many of the members of our company. The bell rings, and the train starts slowly along," wrote an eighteen-year-old Illinois recruit who would soon join Union forces heading for the battlefield.[1]

Such scenes were repeated across the North and the South. In early 1862, the Morgans and numerous other families in Baton Rouge, such as the Garcias, were still confident, but they feared the consequences of armed conflict in their town. When young Céline Garcia's father began preparing for battle, she reported in her journal that "the real war" had begun, but at first "it did not seem very terrible. All the ladies, beautifully dressed, were on the Boulevard and on all the promenade grounds. Every other house, almost, was serenaded. . . . The next day all was laughter and feasting."

The following week, however, the troops were ordered to ship out. They were on their way to fight, and "tears began to flow," Céline wrote.[2]

EARLY ACTIONS

During the early days of the war, the Union began a naval blockade of Confederate ports from Norfolk, Virginia, to Galveston, Texas. The plan was to prevent shipping, particularly exports of Southern cotton to European textile mills, and to cripple the Confederate economy. The Union also planned to divide the Confederacy by controlling the Mississippi River from north to south. Another part of the plan was to control the area west of the Appalachian Mountains in order to cut off access to the eastern war region, which stretched from areas around the U.S. capital in Washington, D.C., to the Confederate capital in Richmond, Virginia.

The Confederacy used a defensive strategy, waiting for attacks and hoping to wear out the Union armies. Early on, General Pierre Beauregard, who had commanded the attack on Fort Sumter, organized troops in Virginia to guard the Confederacy's northern border.

For the first three months of the war, there were minor clashes between Union and Confederate troops in the border states of Missouri and Kentucky and in the western part of Virginia that would soon become the state of West Virginia. But there were no decisive results, and Northerners became impatient. In response to a call for action to bring a quick end to the war, General Irvin McDowell, commander of the main federal army, prepared for an offensive.

In mid-July, McDowell led his troops from outside Washington, D.C., toward the Confederate capital. As the Yankees marched off, their battle cry was "On to Richmond." Rebels countered with "Forward to Washington."

Crowds of civilians, including congressmen and reporters, followed the Union troops. Many people carried picnic lunches with them and watched from atop hills or bluffs as the armies advanced and met in brief skirmishes. It was rather like a moving stage performance with a mass of players in varied "costumes." Many troops had not been issued complete uniforms so they wore their own clothing. Some were decked out in colorful garb such as plaid trousers or broad-brimmed hats with feathers that had been designed earlier for their regiment.

Some families accompanied soldiers on marches, and occasionally wives went into battle with their husbands. A few young women like Kady Brownell held militarylike positions with a regiment. Wearing a uniform and carrying a flag,

The family of this Confederate soldier accompanied him to war and set up housekeeping in a small tent wherever they could.

these women led parades and sometimes marched into battlefields, raising the colors high to rally and guide the troops. Kady and her husband were with a Rhode Island regiment made up of several companies that joined the 33,000 Union troops who marched into Virginia.

As the Federals advanced along dusty roads in the sweltering heat, Rebels stationed at the first outposts retreated. Union forces as well as civilians were confident Richmond would be captured and the war would end quickly. But that was not to be the case.

THE FIRST MAJOR BATTLE

At daybreak on July 21, 1861, the Yanks met 22,000 Rebels near a stream called Bull Run, outside Manassas Junction, a small rail center in northern Virginia. Many witnesses observed and recorded the battle that followed, the first major conflict of the Civil War. (Later, Northerners, who named battles after waterways, called it the First Battle of Bull Run, while Southerners, using place names, called it the First Battle of Manassas.) One eyewitness was Charles Coffin, a newsman for the *Boston Journal*, who reported on the movement of federal troops into combat:

> The Second Rhode Island infantry is . . . deployed as skirmishers. The men are five paces apart. They move slowly, cautiously, and nervously through the fields and thickets. Suddenly, from bushes, trees, and fences there is a rattle of musketry. . . . There are jets of flame and smoke, and a strange humming in the air. There is another rattle, a roll, a volley. The cannon join.[3]

The 1st Rhode Island advanced, with Kady in the lead raising her flag while shells flew overhead, gunfire cracked, and bullets whizzed past. At first, it seemed that the Union would soon claim victory. But as Rebel soldiers fell, replacements quickly appeared, fighting back ferociously.

For hours the battle raged, and men lay "bleeding, torn, and mangled," Coffin wrote, adding that this was "a new, strange, unanticipated experience to the soldiers of both armies, far different from what they thought it would be."[4]

That proved to be quite an understatement. In midafternoon, some of the federal troops broke their line of advance and began to race to the rear. Others followed, with the Confederates right behind. Kady, who stood her ground

Kady Brownell in her Union military uniform

for a time, was forced to retreat when a soldier grabbed her arm and pulled her along.

In panic and confusion, many Union men dropped their weapons and threw off canteens, blankets, and anything else that might slow down their flight. The Confederates in pursuit stopped to pick up much of the equipment and, due to inexperience, allowed the retreating Federals to find refuge back in Washington. Nevertheless, for the Confederates, it was "a great victory—a thorough *rout*," wrote Mary Chesnut, wife of a U.S. senator who had resigned to aid the Confederacy. Early in the war, Mary Chesnut had started a diary, which was to become one of the most famous of the period. Although grateful for the victory and the safety of those close to her, she was distressed by the "dead & dying strewing the fields."[5] Both sides suffered many casualties.

ANOTHER UNION RETREAT

Northerners were not only saddened but also discouraged by the outcome of Bull Run. As the Indiana farm boy Theodore Upson noted, "We got whipped all right and no mistake. Some folks feel pretty blue."[6]

Within a few days, President Lincoln put a new commander in charge, General George B. McClellan, who began to develop a more disciplined army. He trained and drilled his soldiers for months in preparation for an attack on Richmond. In March 1862, McClellan's forces sailed from Washington down the Potomac River, into Chesapeake Bay. They landed in April on a peninsula between the York and James Rivers and occupied Yorktown, southeast of Richmond.

McClellan could not sail up the James River to Richmond because it was blocked by a Confederate ironclad

President Lincoln visited General McClellan at his field headquarters.

ship, the *Virginia.* Formerly the *Merrimack,* the ship had been taken over months before by Confederates at Norfolk and refurbished with a covering of iron plates, making it resistant to attack. The *Virginia* had already destroyed several ships in the Union navy, and before McClellan's arrival, had battled the Union's ironclad, the *Monitor,* although neither ship was damaged.

Once at Yorktown, McClellan moved his force of 100,000 up the peninsula by land. But Union troops were stopped 9 miles (15 kilometers) from Richmond in a battle that resulted in severe wounds for Confederate General Joseph E. Johnston. The famed General Robert E. Lee took over the command of the Confederate army and, along with another famous general, Thomas J. "Stonewall" Jackson, began to surround McClellan's men. After what became known as the Seven Days battles, from June 25 to July 1, McClellan was forced to retreat.

While Union troops waited to leave the peninsula and return north, reinforcements arrived, but they were too late to be of any help. One Indiana soldier who was among the reinforcement troops wrote a letter to his sister explaining that "ever thing is quiet along the whole line. The Secesh [secessionists] has fallen back I dont know how far though." Then he described one of the inconsistencies of the war: "When we first came here our pickets [patrols or guards] and the secesh pickets were not more than 150 yds apart. Sometimes our boys and the secesh would lay down their guns and meet half way and talk for an hour perhaps."[7]

WAR ON MANY FRONTS

Although the Union suffered setbacks in the East, federal troops staged offensives on several fronts. They stopped Confederate ships that tried to break through the blockade along the coast and at the mouth of the Mississippi River. During February 1862, federal troops led by General Ulysses S. Grant captured two forts on waterways that emptied into the Mississippi. Capturing the forts helped protect portions of the river highways used for transportation of troops and supplies.

Then Grant and his troops started south to take over other posts on the Mississippi. They camped for a time at Pittsburg Landing, Tennessee, to wait for another federal army, under General Don Carlos Buell, to join them. Grant believed the Confederates, who usually planned defensively, would be preparing for the Union advance. Security was lax,

General Grant captured two forts on waterways
with the aid of gunboats similar to this one.

and the federal camp spread out over a large area near a meetinghouse called Shiloh Church.

Before Buell arrived, the Confederates surprised Grant, and the two-day battle that followed is considered one of the bloodiest of any American war. Although the Confederates were successful the first day, their commander was killed, creating some confusion. The troops were also exhausted. So when Buell's army appeared on the second day in midafternoon, the battle changed—"It was the last struggle of the Confederates, ending in defeat," as one Confederate soldier, John S. Jackman, wrote in his diary.

The Shiloh battle resulted in thousands of dead and wounded. Jackman noted that Confederate wounded who were "not able to walk, were placed in wagons, and started for Corinth"[8] in Mississippi near the border with Tennessee. It was there that the Confederates pulled back to regroup and plan their next move.

Four

✷

MOUNTING DEATH TOLLS

The 27th Tennessee lost over half of their force at Shiloh. Six months later, at Perryville, Kentucky, the same regiment was cut in half once again. Such a situation was common during the entire course of this bloody conflict. Counting both Yankee and Rebel armies, 115 regiments lost at least half of their men in a single battle. One Union regiment (at Gettysburg) and one Confederate regiment (at Antietam) reported losses of over 80 percent of their men.

Statistics show the magnitude of the Civil War carnage. More than 600,000 Americans died in this war—a death toll higher than the combined U.S. deaths in all wars from the Revolution through the Korean conflict. While the Civil War battle losses were high, twice as many men died from illness and disease as they did from gunfire and cannon shot. Smallpox, measles, pneumonia, and gastric problems ran amok because of the deplorable conditions both armies had to endure. For instance, diarrhea alone killed more than 30,000 Union soldiers.

DEATH FROM DISEASE

At the time of the Civil War, scientific knowledge was limited and medical practices were still mostly experimental. Hospitals were crowded, unsanitary places. Thus soldiers who contracted malaria, smallpox, or one of the other common diseases of the day were at great risk; chances for survival were poor to none. Intestinal diseases seemed to be the worst complaint of soldiers.

"There is but one kind of Sickness here, and that is the diarhoea, and everybody has it," wrote one Union soldier. Another noted in a diary that he was "sick with diarhea. Sickest I ever was."[1]

Some of the soldiers who suffered this discomfort, which they called "the quickstep," treated themselves. Captain Edward Redington of the 28th Wisconsin, for example, described in his log how he discovered a cure:

I have been taking quinine, pain-killer, and whiskey and my head feels rather large and rings like a kettle. The way they all got mixed up was in this way: a bottle of quinine and pain-killer got broken in my medicine chest; the quinine soaking up the pain-killer, so I put them in another bottle and filled up with whiskey. A more villainous compound to swallow never passed a man's lips. I have given several of the boys out of the same bottle and it has always cured them without fail. I think I shall apply for a patent on it as a cure for all the ills the flesh is heir to from colic to cholera.[2]

SCARCE SUPPLIES, LITTLE MONEY

The scarcity of food and supplies in both the North and South contributed to the ill health of the troops. The Confederates especially lacked many basic necessities, such as tents and shoes. Financing the war and supplying a massive number of troops were of constant concern to the Rebel leaders. Soldiers often wrote about the problems of just getting by to fight another day. One described the trials and difficulties of his regiment:

These Confederate soldiers were among the many who had no uniforms.

> We were for days without a morsel of food, excepting occasionally a meal of parched corn. . . . The men on the march ran through the gardens . . . devouring every particle of vegetables like the army worm leaving nothing at all standing. Whenever a cow or hog were found it was shot down & soon dispatched.[3]

Another Confederate noted, "Our army is almost starved out. Our rations has been Beef and flour since we left Richmond and not more than half enough of that many times we had Green Corn and apples issued to us and were glad of that." One man reported that when his company obtained a young calf, the first beef they had seen for weeks, "We ate it raw, without salt or bread." And a South Carolina colonel commented that he "frequently saw the hungry Confederate gather up the dirt and corn where a horse had been fed, so that when he reached his bivouac he could wash out the dirt and gather the few grains of corn to satisfy in part at least the cravings of hunger."[4]

THREATS FROM MOSQUITOES

William Poague with the Army of Northern Virginia, wrote to his relatives about another hazard of war—disease-carrying

Netting was provided for patients in this Civil War hospital to protect them from disease-carrying mosquitoes.

mosquitoes, which he claimed were a worse foe than the Yankees. As he explained in a letter home:

> I have heard many musquitoe yarns and storys but I believe they all fall short of the realities I have experienced in the past two weeks....An officer who is located near me here sends the worst cases he has for punishment to the picket lines in the swamp to fight and be fought by, not Yankees but musquitoes. They are not allowed to take their guns lest shooting at and being shot at by the Yankees might divert their minds from their agony.[5]

THE DEADLIEST BATTLE

In spite of horrible living conditions, some of the worst moments of the war took place on the battlefields. After the Confederate victories at Bull Run (Manassas) and against McClellan on the Yorktown peninsula, there was a second battle at Bull Run in August 1862. Once again the federal troops were stopped, and they retreated to Washington, D.C. Virginia was now clear of federal forces.

Confederate wounded in Virginia waiting for transportation to hospitals

General Robert E. Lee decided that the time was right to invade the North. By gaining a victory there, he hoped that the Confederacy would be seen as a legitimate power in the eyes of the English and French governments. Recognition as a lawful country by these two nations could bring supplies and money to continue the war effort.

Lee's regiments waded across the Potomac River on September 5, 1862. Lincoln sent McClellan to confront the Rebels, and a great battle took place at Antietam Creek in Maryland on September 17. Throughout the day, federal troops battered the Rebel lines. McClellan never sent his superior forces in a mass attack, but instead ordered separate attacks up and down the line. Casualties mounted at an alarming rate. By nightfall, Lee's army still held its position. On both sides, thousands were wounded or killed.

From a military point of view, the result was a standoff, but from a political perspective it was the turning point of the war. Lee had to retreat to Virginia without his victory, and on September 22, President Abraham Lincoln issued his Preliminary Emancipation Proclamation, or formal statement declaring that slaves within Rebel states would be free on January 1, 1863.

Five

EMANCIPATION AND REBELLION

Since the beginning of the war, the president had been trying to bolster support for the military effort. His stated goal was to bring the Confederate states back into the Union, but many Northerners did not care if the South ever rejoined the United States. By emancipating the slaves held in Confederate territory, Lincoln hoped to put the reason for the war on a "moral" footing. He altered the war into a struggle for human freedom, and in this manner gained some citizen support. More important, European nations began to see the fight for the Union as somehow more than just the issues of the Confederate states, and Europeans were not as inclined to recognize or support the Confederate States of America.

On January 1, 1863, Lincoln's Emancipation Proclamation went into effect, declaring that "all persons held as slaves within any State or designated part of a State . . . in rebellion against the United States shall be then, thenceforward, and forever free." The proclamation did *not*, however, offer freedom to slaves in states or sections of states that were not part of the Confederacy. Freeing the slaves in Rebel states angered Southern whites, who were convinced that Lincoln was intent on destroying their way of life. The Rebels were even more determined to fight on, no matter what the cost. Reunion with the federal government would be like no life at all.

THE FIGHTING 54TH

Under the terms of the Emancipation Proclamation, the North began organizing regiments of ex-slaves and other free blacks. Initially, the plan was to have these troops perform duties behind the fighting lines, since whites generally believed that blacks did not have the courage to fight. But it soon became clear that the blacks were as brave and skilled as other Union soldiers.

About 186,000 blacks served in the Union army. One of the first fighting regiments was the 54th Massachusetts Volunteers. For one year during the war, the 54th protested discrimination by refusing to accept unequal pay—by law, black privates were paid $10 per month but $3 was deducted for clothing; in contrast, white privates received $13 *plus* clothing.

One member of the "glorious 54th," as it became known, was Corporal James Henry Gooding, who wrote letters that were published in the *New Bedford* (Massachusetts) *Mercury*, his hometown paper. After months of recruiting and training, Gooding reported on May 24, 1863, "We have received our marching orders; . . . so next Sunday I think we shall be on our way to Dixie. . . . The citizens of this Commonwealth need not be ashamed of the 54th now; and if the regiment will be allowed a chance, I feel confident the Coloured Volunteers will add glory to her already bright name." [1]

Their chance was to come very quickly. On July 18, 1863, Company C of the 54th Massachusetts Volunteers led a charge into some of the deadliest fire of the war. The 54th was on Morris Island at the entrance of South Carolina's Charleston harbor. The regiment was part of a concentration

The 54th Massachusetts was a regiment of black volunteers that came to be known as the "glorious 54th" because of their bravery.

of forces making the first assault to open up the route to capture the city of Charleston. Fort Wagner was a heavily fortified site on the island that had been first attacked by Union troops on July 10. Some ground had been gained, and further attack was up a sandy, narrow beach and over an embankment that would expose any advancing troops to a hail of Rebel lead. The 54th Massachusetts arrived July 18 after fighting its way through another island, sleeping little in three days, and not eating for twenty-four hours. Regardless, the men volunteered to lead the frontal assault.

Corporal Gooding reported in a letter that

Gen'l Strong asked us if we would follow him into Fort Wagner. Every man said, yes—we were ready to follow wherever we were led.... we went at it, over the ditch and on to the parapet through a deadly fire; but we could not get into the fort. We met the foe on the parapet of Wagner with the bayonet—we were exposed to a murderous fire from the batteries of the fort, from our Monitors [ironclad gunboats] and our land batteries, as they did not cease firing soon enough. Mortal men could not stand such a fire.[2]

After the exploits of the men of the 54th became known, the black soldier's courage and loyalty was clearly evident. As the *New York Tribune* noted, "It made Fort Wagner such a name to the colored race as Bunker Hill has been for ninety years to the white Yankees."[3] Yet the majority of whites in the North did not hold people of color in high esteem. Like their Southern counterparts, most were convinced that blacks were inferior to whites, and they could see no good reason to die in a war for black freedom.

DRAFT RIOTS

That attitude had prevailed from the beginning of the war, and with battle losses and many casualties throughout 1862, support for the military effort waned. President Lincoln pleaded for Union volunteers and eventually ordered governors to draft men into the state militias. In March 1863, the U.S. Congress authorized a military draft requiring all able-bodied male citizens between the ages of twenty and forty-five to join the armed forces.

Poor Northern white men, especially Irish immigrants, resented the idea of forced military service. The system, after all, was hardly fair. For $300, a man could pay a substitute to take his place in the draft. But the average yearly wage was

Mobs protesting the draft rioted in New York City.

only $500. Thus the rich were able to stay home, while the poor had to fight.

Resentment against this system came to a head in July 1863, when riots in protest of the draft broke out in Boston, Massachusetts, and Troy, New York. Other cities, including Chicago, and parts of Vermont and Pennsylvania also saw violence. But the worst started in the poor Irish neighborhood of New York City. Here a mob set a recruiting office afire, then turned on the black population, claiming the freed slaves were trying to take their jobs.

Rioting lasted for four days, with race the central issue. Abolitionists' homes were destroyed and the Coloured Orphan Asylum was torched. In all, more than 1,000 people were killed and many more wounded. At least a dozen blacks were hanged by crazed white rioters. Army troops were called in to finally help regain the peace.

Six

CONTINUED FIGHTING AND DEVASTATION

After Stonewall Jackson stopped a federal advance at Chancellorsville, Virginia, in May of 1863, General Lee decided that it was time to make a second try at invading Northern territory. For one thing, he knew that General Ulysses S. Grant was putting heavy pressure on the citizens of Vicksburg, Mississippi, in the West. Lee also wanted to engage the Yankees outside of Virginia, and he hoped to capture some sorely needed federal supplies. In June, he crossed the Potomac with a force of 75,000 men.

The federal troops, whose strength was at 90,000, were led by General George G. Meade, a newly appointed commander selected by Lincoln to chase down the Confederates under Lee. Scouting parties from the two forces met in a small skirmish near the town of Gettysburg, Pennsylvania, the morning of July 1. The generals then quickly concentrated their men in preparation for a series of fights that lasted for three days.

By the second day, it appeared the Confederates would win the battle, but due to the bravery of many Union soldiers, their positions held. One commander given the job of defending a critical piece of land was Colonel Joshua Chamberlain. He recounted the events of July 2 as his men defended the left flank of the Union army:

Joshua L. Chamberlain is shown here wearing the brigadier general's star he won on the battlefield.

Finding myself unable to hold it by the mere defensive, after more than a third of my men had fallen, and my ammunition was exhausted ... and having at that moment right upon me a third desperate onset of the enemy with more than three times my numbers, I saw no way to hold the position but to make a countercharge with the bayonet, and to place myself at the head of it. ... We cleared the enemy entirely from the left flank of our lines ... and brought back from our charge twice as many prisoners as the entire number of men in our own ranks.[1]

Then, on the last day, after a lengthy Confederate artillery pounding, 12,000 Rebel infantrymen under General George Pickett assaulted the Union positions on Cemetery Ridge. The charge was repulsed under the weight of Union shot, shell, and bayonet. But losses to both sides (killed, wounded, and missing in the battle of Gettysburg) were estimated at over 50,000 men and boys. Although the fighting in

A memorial to the 1st Pennsylvania Cavalry that fought at Gettysburg

the East continued for almost two years, the Confederates never really recovered from the loss at Gettysburg. At the same time, in the West, another major turning point in the war took place.

ATTACKS ON VICKSBURG

Ulysses Grant, in command of the Union army in the West, was fresh from a victory at Shiloh when he headed for Vicksburg. Strategically located on the Mississippi River, Vicksburg was occupied by a large force of Confederate soldiers under the command of Lieutenant General John C. Pemberton. From Vicksburg, Pemberton could control the flow of arms and supplies on that part of the river. So it was very important that Grant capture the city.

The city sat high on a bank with a commanding view of any troops who might try to scale the heights. Since an attack from the river was out of the question, Grant attacked from the south and west, but his men were repulsed.

A farmer from Pennsylvania who was fighting with the Union troops recalled what happened next: "On May 22, 1863, when Grant made his second attack on Vicksburg, Colonel Coleman called for volunteers to go ahead of the main column with scaling ladders and guns, and storm the works in front of Vicksburg. I was one of the 226 that volunteered."

Another volunteer told of the terrible fire they endured in that mission. He recounted, "I had 21 bullets through my clothes, three through my hat, and nary a one touched the hide." Others weren't so lucky. As a volunteer reported, "Only 20 of us got back alive."[2]

Some men reached the objective: a Confederate fort. The Union soldiers were supposed to keep the enemy from firing the fort's large guns at the advancing troops, but the forces that were to follow them could not get through. This left the forward squad stranded. Joseph Labille of the 6th Missouri described what it was like:

> We lay flat on the top [of the fort roof] . . . in the hot burning sun within 3 or 4 feet of the enemy, keeping them from firing their cannons. . . . Sometime in the afternoon our army made the charge but did not succeed in reaching us, though we kept the fort silent. . . . We remained there until dark. . . . I do not know how the other boys got back but I got across the ditch and jumped a fence. . . . I was reported killed but the boys were happy to see me alive again."[3]

UNDER SIEGE

Even before General Grant's unsuccessful attempts to capture Vicksburg, he had ordered his troops to surround the town and lay siege. That is, the federal soldiers planned to capture the town by keeping out supplies and starving residents so that they would surrender. In this case, the siege lasted for more than a month. During that time, the Union troops constantly bombarded the residents with cannon and mortar fire.

A mother of a two-year-old child whose husband was assigned to Vicksburg kept a diary of events that transpired there during the siege. While her husband was with the

The Union could supply its army for a long siege because
it had large stockpiles of weapons and ammunition.

Rebel troops, she, her baby, and their servants stayed at home in town. Mortar fire became so intense and dangerous, however, that she, like most townspeople, had to take refuge in caves that had been dug into the city's hills and embankments. This young woman, known only as "a Lady," explained the situation:

> Caves were the fashion—the rage—over besieged Vicksburg. Negroes who understood their business, hired themselves out to dig them, at thirty to fifty dollars, according to size. Many persons, considering different localities unsafe, would sell them to others, who had been less fortunate, or less provident; and so great was the demand for cave workmen, that a new branch of industry sprang up.[4]

The Lady went on to describe her "new habitation . . . an excavation made in the earth, and branching six feet from the entrance, forming a cave in the shape of a T. In one of the wings my bed fitted; the other I used as a kind of dressing room."[5]

The siege of Vicksburg forced many of the townspeople into caves dug into the hills.

The Confederate defenders, though numbering more than 29,000 with 132 cannon and some 50,000 other weapons, could do very little against the constant barrage of cannon fire. The Lady continued her description of life in her once secure city:

> One afternoon, amid the rush and explosion of the shells, cries and screams arose—the screams of women amid the shrieks of the falling shells. The servant boy, George, after starting and coming back once or twice ... at last gathered courage to go to the ravine near us, from whence the cries proceeded; and found that a negro man had been buried alive within a cave.... This incident made me doubly doubtful about my cave; I feared that I might be buried alive at any-time.[6]

By the beginning of July, the situation in Vicksburg had become desperate. Pemberton, the military commander, knew that the citizens were facing death from starvation or falling shells. On July 4, 1863, he surrendered the city, his men, and all of their arms. This loss was a terrible blow to the Confederates. A huge force of men was lost, opening a gateway for Union entry into the heart of Dixie.

Seven

MISERY TO THE END

In February of 1864, James Gooding, who had survived the shells and bullets at Fort Wagner, was seriously wounded in the battle of Olustee, Florida. He was captured there and transported to Andersonville Prison in Georgia. Andersonville was the most vile prison of the Confederate states. About 45,000 men were crowded into a very small space that contained almost no buildings, no sanitation facilities, and little food. Prisoners received their drinking water from a small stream that ran through the camp. The stream was also used for bathing and as a toilet.

Because of the filth and exposure to the elements, disease was everywhere. Corporal Gooding soon died in Andersonville. He was among nearly 13,000 Union prisoners who met their deaths in the nine months the prison operated. If they were able to survive the ordeal, most of the captured men looked like living skeletons at the end of the war.

One new arrival wrote:

> since the day I was Born I never saw such misery as there is here.... they can't get aney soap or aney thing else to wash their clothes with.... us Boys got a spade & took off the top of the ground & it was alive with maggots where we Lay.... there isn't a Hog ste in the North aney nastier than this camp.[1]

John Ransom of Michigan complained too: "There is so much filth about the camp that it is terrible trying to live here. . . . With sunken eyes, blackened countenances from pitch pine smoke, rags and disease, the men look sickening. The air reeks of nastiness."[2]

Food was in very short supply, contributing to the weakened condition of the prison population. The Rebels claimed that the small rations for the Union soldiers were exactly what the Southern soldiers were given: supplies were just that low. But the Union authorities did not believe this. They retaliated by cutting the rations of Southern prisoners who were held in Union camps, which like Andersonville lacked facilities and comfort.

Henry Handerson recounted that the food was "mighty appalling" when he was first captured by the Union troops who had decided to set up a camp on Morris Island. It was a place where prisoners were deliberately exposed to the cannonade of the Confederate batteries some distance away. Though no one was injured by cannon fire, Handerson wrote that

> the same cannot be said of the diet and the water furnished by our enemies. Our sole supply of water was procured from a shallow hole dug in the sandy beach. . . . it was always scanty in quantity, warm and unrefreshing. Nor was our food any better. The latter consisted chiefly of boiled rice and bean soup. . . . The rice was usually full of worms, whose palatability was not materially improved by boiling.[3]

CAPTURED SPIES

Among the prisoners of war on both sides were many citizens who were spies. Thousands took part in espionage as a way to help their cause—whether for the Union or the Confederacy—and some spies became famous for their exploits and daring escapes from prison.

A Civil War prison camp in Elmira, New York, held more than 12,000 Confederate prisoners. By July 1865, almost 3,000 had died mainly because of poor conditions at the camp.

Numerous spies were women, among them Belle Boyd, who lived in the Shenandoah Valley near Harpers Ferry, Virginia. Boyd spied for the Confederates during most of the Civil War, gathering information about federal military activities, which she forwarded in code to Rebel forces.

Women in espionage often disguised themselves as men in order to infiltrate the enemy's army. One such woman was Emma Edmonds, whose boyfriend died early in the war while riding the picket line for the Union. Seeking revenge against the Rebels, she volunteered to be a Union spy. She not only played the role of a male Rebel soldier, but also darkened her skin and wore a wig to masquerade as a black man.

Edmonds became part of a black work crew digging trenches and building embankments of dirt 8 feet (2.4 meters) high for Rebel defenses in Richmond. In a book about her experiences, she noted that the "work was exceed-

Emma Edmonds was a famous spy for the Union during the Civil War.

ingly hard for the strongest man," but the laborers helped one another. She was able to trade off on occasion with workers who had lighter jobs, such as carrying water for the troops. Once when she brought a fresh supply of water to the army post, she reported:

> I saw a group of soldiers gathered around some individual who was haranguing them.... I thought the voice sounded familiar, and upon taking a sly look at the speaker I recognized him at once as a peddler who used to come to the Federal camp regularly once every week with newspapers and stationery.... He would hang around there, under some pretext or other, for half a day at a time.[4]

The peddler turned out to be a spy for the Rebels. According to Edmonds, he gave the Confederates "a full description of our camp and forces, and also brought out a map of the entire works of McClellan's position." From that point on, the Rebel spy "was a fated man. . . . His life was not worth three cents,"[5] Edmonds wrote. Within a few days, she was able to return to the federal side and report to General McClellan's headquarters.

MULTIPLE ATTACKS ON THE CONFEDERACY

In 1864, President Lincoln named General Ulysses S. Grant general-in-chief, responsible for all the Union armies. Grant began preparations to strangle the Confederacy. He ordered concurrent attacks at significant positions in the Southern states, and federal troops hammered away on the weakened Rebel forces.

Early in May 1864, General Grant with 119,000 men marched toward Richmond, expecting to overpower the poorly armed and smaller Confederate army of just 64,000 men. Grant expected to occupy the Confederate capital. But General Robert E. Lee, who commanded the Confederate forces, was able to fend off Grant's men during their advance through Virginia. Tens of thousands died in battles along the way. But Grant pressed on, changing his strategy and marching his men to the southeast of Richmond and eventually setting up a siege of Petersburg, which continued until the end of the war.

During the siege, Grant slowly extended his troops, moving them farther to the south and west. As a result, Lee had to set up defenses, stretching his troops and resources to near the breaking point.

Meanwhile, other federal forces had been attacking in Tennessee, Alabama, and Georgia. In the spring of 1864, General William Tecumseh Sherman carried out a campaign through Georgia that ended late in the year with Sherman's march to the sea. As his Union army moved southeast, soldiers tore up rail lines in order to prevent supplies from reaching Rebel troops. They also looted and destroyed homes from Atlanta to Savannah.

The farm boy Theodore Upson, who at age sixteen joined the Indiana 100th Regiment, became one of Sherman's scouts. In a journal about his experiences, he reported that when federal troops reached Atlanta in the fall of 1864, they "utterly destroyed" the city. "I don't think any people will want to try and live there now. It is pretty tough to rout people out of their homes in this way, but it is war, and General Sherman is credited with saying that 'War Is Hell.' I think that it is."[6]

All residents of Atlanta were forced to leave and Sherman ordered his troops to burn the city to the ground. Then Sherman led his men southeast toward the seaport of Savannah. The main purpose of the march was to destroy food supplies that the Confederate army needed and to discourage citizens from continuing the war. Troops foraged for food and then burned the land along their way. People were too frightened to resist. As Upson explained, "We have had but little

General Sherman's Union soldiers looted and destroyed many homes in their path when they marched through Georgia.

opposition so far—now and then a few Cavelry at some cross roads or at a stream. But in a few minutes they . . . scatter."[7]

Sometimes, of course, there were severe encounters and losses among both Confederate and Union troops. After one battle prior to the attack on Atlanta, Upson lost a close friend and helped bury him and other Union soldiers who died in battle. Then he went to the front line, where he saw the Confederate dead:

It was a terrible sight. Some one was groaning. We moved a few bodies, and there was a boy with a broken arm and leg—just a boy 14 years old; and beside him, cold in death, lay his Father, two Brothers, and an Uncle. It was a harvest of death. We brought the poor fellow up to the fire. Our surgeons made him as comfortable as they could. Then we marched away leaving him with his own wounded who we could no longer care for.[8]

Sherman and his troops occupied Savannah in late December 1864. As the new year began, some Confederate forces were intact in Mississippi and Alabama, but the Confederate states had dwindled to only the Carolinas and the southern half of Virginia. Union leaders were certain that the end of the war was near.

SURRENDER

Sherman's army marched north through the Carolinas to meet Grant's forces in Virginia in the spring of 1865. The Confederates could offer only minor resistance. Lee and his men, ragged and many of them barefoot, made a desperate attempt in March to stop the Union army before it reached Petersburg, just south of Richmond. The effort failed, and Grant's troops occupied the city on April 2, then moved on to the Confederate capital, forcing President Davis to flee. As Confederate troops left the city, they set fire to military buildings. The flames spread, destroying Richmond.

Within days, Lee decided that the South would be completely wiped out if he did not surrender. He sent word to Grant that he would meet him at Appomattox Court House, a town in southern Virginia. On April 9, 1865, Confederate General Robert E. Lee surrendered his army to Union General Ulysses S. Grant, and the Civil War for the most part was over. Rebel armies farther south and some west of the Mississippi River surrendered over the next two months, and the Confederate resistance ended.

But the hatred and killing did not stop. Just five days after Lee's surrender, on April 14, President Abraham Lincoln was shot to death by a fanatic. Lincoln's murder deeply affected Union soldiers. As George Putnam, a Union officer, wrote years after the war, "I found myself . . . in the crowd of ten thousand men all overpowered by the same emotion. Never before had I seen thousands of grown men sobbing together."[9]

The Yankees were not alone in their sorrow and sense of loss. Years later, many in the South realized that Lincoln would likely have advocated government policies to help rebuild the devastated Southern communities in an orderly fashion. He might also have been able to encourage Americans to follow the advice he gave in his second inaugural address—to act "with malice toward none; with charity for all."

Source Notes

One

1. Céline Fremaux Garcia, *Céline: Remembering Louisiana, 1850–1871*, ed. Patrick J. Geary (Athens, Ga.: University of Georgia Press, 1987), 62.
2. Theodore D. Weld, *American Slavery As It Is: Testimony of a Thousand Witnesses, in Leslie H. Fishel, Jr.*, and Benjamin Quarles, *The Negro American: A Documentary History* (Glenview, Ill.: Scott, Foresman, 1967), 185.
3. Charlotte Forten, diary, in Fishel and Quarles, *Negro American*, 201–202.
4. Garcia, *Céline: Remembering Louisiana*, 64.

Two

1. Quoted in James M. McPherson, *The Negro's Civil War: How American Negroes Felt and Acted during the War for the Union* (Urbana, Ill.: University of Illinois Press, 1982), 5.
2. Theodore F. Upson, *With Sherman to the Sea: The Civil War Letters Diaries and Reminiscences of Theodore F. Upson*, ed. Oscar Osburn Winther (Bloomington, Ind.: Indiana University Press, 1958), 8.
3. Ibid.
4. Quoted in Samuel Eliot Morrison, *The Oxford History of the American People* (New York: Oxford University Press, 1965), 610.
5. Upson, *With Sherman to the Sea*, 9.
6. Ibid., 11.
7. Alfred M. Green, *Letters and Discussions on the Formation of Colored Regiments, and the Duty of the Colored People*

in Regard to the Great Slaveholder's Rebellion, in the United States of America (Philadelphia: Ringwalt and Brown, 1862), 3.

8. Sarah Morgan Dawson, *A Confederate Girl's Diary*, ed. James I. Robertson, Jr. (Bloomington, Ind.: Indiana University Press, 1960), 31.

9. Ibid., 32.

Three

1. B. T. Smith, *Private Smith's Journal: Recollections of the Late War*, ed. Clyde C. Walton (Chicago: R. R. Donnelly and Sons, 1963), 11.

2. Garcia, *Céline: Remembering Louisiana*, 66.

3. Quoted in Richard Wheeler, *Voices of the Civil War* (New York: Thomas Y. Crowell, 1976), 32–33.

4. Ibid., 34.

5. Mary Boykin Miller Chesnut, *The Private Mary Chesnut: The Unpublished Civil War Diaries*, ed. C. Vann Woodward and Elisabeth Muhlenfeld (New York: Oxford University Press, 1984), 100.

6. Upson, *With Sherman to the Sea*, 11.

7. Quoted in Nancy Niblack Baxter, ed., *Hoosier Farmboy in Lincoln's Army: The Civil War Letters of Pvt. John R. McClure of the 14th Indiana Regiment* (Indianapolis: Guild Press of Indiana, 1992), 27.

8. John S. Jackman, *Diary of a Confederate Soldier: John S. Jackman of the Orphan Brigade*, ed. William C. Davis (Columbia, S.C.: University of South Carolina Press, 1990), 32.

Four

1. Quoted in Bell Irvin Wiley, *The Life of Billy Yank: The Common Soldier of the Union* (Baton Rouge: Louisiana State University Press, 1992, original printing 1957), 136.

2. Ibid., 139.

3. Quoted in Bell Irvin Wiley, *The Life of Johnny Reb: The Common Soldier of the Confederacy* (Baton Rouge: Louisiana State University Press, 1992, originally published 1943), 92.

4. Ibid., 93.

5. William Thomas Poague, *Gunner with Stonewall: Reminiscences of William Thomas Poague*, ed. Monroe F. Cockrell (Jackson, Tenn.: McCowat-Mercer Press, 1957), 137.

Five

1. James Henry Gooding, *On the Altar of Freedom: A Black Soldier's Civil War Letters from the Front*, ed. Virginia M. Adams (New York: Warner Books, 1991), 24.

2. Ibid., 38.

3. Ibid., xii.

Six

1. Quoted in Joseph B. Mitchell, *The Badge of Gallantry: Recollections of Civil War Congressional Medal of Honor Winners, Letters from the Charles Kohen Collection* (New York: Macmillan, 1965), 130.

2. Ibid., 115.

3. Ibid., 113–114.

4. *My Cave Life in Vicksburg, with Letters of Trial and Travel, by a Lady* (New York: D. Appleton and Company, 1864), 72.

5. Ibid., 61.

6. Ibid., 63.

Seven

1. Quoted in Ovid L. Futch, *History of Andersonville Prison* (Hialeah, Fla.: Board of Commissioners of State Institution of Florida, University of Florida Press, 1968), 39.

2. Ibid., 10.

3. Henry E. Handerson, *Yankee in Gray: The Civil War Memoirs of Henry E. Handerson with a Selection of His Wartime Letters* (Cleveland: Press of Western Reserve University, 1962), 77.

4. Quoted in Philip Van Doren Stern, *Secret Missions of the Civil War* (Chicago: Rand, McNally and Company, 1959), 127.

5. Ibid., 128.

6. Upson, *With Sherman to the Sea*, 133.

7. Ibid., 134.

8. Ibid., 38.

9. George Haven Putnam, *A Prisoner of War in Virginia 1864–5* (New York: G. P. Putnam's Sons, 1912), 103.

Further Reading

Biel, Timothy. *The Civil War.* San Diego: Lucent, 1991.

Cannon, Marian G. *Robert E. Lee: Defender of the South.* New York: Watts, 1993.

Carter, Alden R. *The Civil War: American Tragedy.* New York: Watts, 1993.

Chang, Ina. *A Separate Battle: Women and the Civil War.* New York: Dutton, 1991.

Durwood, Thomas A., et al. *The History of the Civil War Series.* Morristown, N.J.: Silver Burdett, 1990.

Katz, William L. *Breaking the Chains: African-American Slave Resistance.* New York: Atheneum, 1990.

Marrin, Albert. *Unconditional Surrender: U.S. Grant and the Civil War.* New York: Atheneum, 1994.

———. *Virginia's General: Robert E. Lee and the Civil War.* New York: Atheneum, 1994.

Mettger, Zak. *Till Victory Is Won: Black Soldiers in the Civil War.* New York: Dutton, 1994.

Murphy, Jim. *The Boy's War: Confederate and Union Soldiers Talk about the Civil War.* Boston: Clarion, 1990.

Reef, Catherine. *The Buffalo Soldiers.* New York: Twenty-First Century Books, 1993.

Steins, Richard. *The Nation Divides: The Civil War.* New York: Twenty-First Century Books, 1993.

Tracey, Patrick. *Military Leaders of the Civil War.* New York: Facts on File, 1993.

Index